ALL IN ALL

Also by Arlene Pollack

Flamencos
Persons, Places, & Things

ALL IN ALL

Stories and Poems

Arlene Pollack

FCP

Full Court Press
Englewood Cliffs, New Jersey

First Edition

Copyright © 2015 by Arlene Pollack

Published in the United States of America
by Full Court Press, 601 Palisade Avenue
Englewood Cliffs, NJ 07632
fullcourtpressnj.com

ISBN 978-1-938812-58-3
Library of Congress Control No. 2015938297

*Editing and Book Design by Barry Sheinkopf
for Bookshapers (bookshapers.com)*

Cover Art by Howard Pollack

Colophon by Liz Sedlack

To Howard Merrill Pollack
my sterling spouse

and

To our family
of six exceptional siblings, their five highly successful
husbands, our nine brilliant grandchildren, one
promising grandson-in-law, and two
great-grandchildren (too young to be classified
but presently quite cute).

Table of Contents

THE PLAYER

"C'MON, ARLENE. PLAY 'SMOKE GETS IN YOUR EYES'."

"But, Daddy . . . "

"Aw, c'mon.. It's my favorite."

I play it.

Daddy beams. "That's a beautiful song."

It's a Saturday afternoon.. We're walking home after seeing a matinée at the Elsmere Theatre. It was a swell picture, with Jeanette MacDonald and Nelson Eddy. We're not talking, because we're still in the picture, if you know what I mean.

Then Daddy hums something from the movie. "Bet you can't play this song . . . "

"Sing it again, Daddy."

"Okay, now listen." Daddy hums it again. He has such a fine voice, as good as any real singer.

We get home and go into the living room. I sit down at the piano. Daddy stands next to me. This is serious business for both of us. He starts humming a few lines of the melody. "Go ahead," he says. So I put my finger on the C to hear if it's possible to build the melody. Nope. Up two notes, and it comes to me. I get almost through what he's sung and now I'm stumped. I try one, two notes down from where I've lost it, but it's gone.

"I can't get that part," I mumble, thinking about it.

"You almost got it. It goes up . . . like this . . . "

He sings the melody again. He's not teaching me; he's just singing because he's working it out, just like I am.

"Wait a minute, Daddy. You're going too fast. I have to try it before I lose the whole thing."

So he waits while I start the part. When I get to the place where I went down instead of up, he sings along with the piano to help me get it right. This time I do get it right, and it's in there forever, in my head.

"Okay. That's it. Start it from the beginning." My father is relieved, as if we've both solved a hard math problem.

"What comes next?" I ask, ready to go.

"Listen." Dad does the next part. It's still the *verse*, the introduction that hardly anyone ever sings. But we always learn it straight through from beginning to end. We like the introductions because they set the scene for the song. They tell the background story. The rest of the song is ordinary by comparison. For instance, take, "You Made Me Love You." The opening goes like this:

> *I've been worried all night long.*
> *Don"t know if I'm right or wrong.*
> *I don't know just what to say.*
> *Your love's made me feel this way.*
> *Why, oh why, should I feel blue?*
> *Once I was in love with you.*
> *But now I'm crying.*
> *No use denying,*
> *There's no one else on earth that'll do.*

Then it goes into the *release*, the part most people sing.
You made me love you.
I didn't wanna do it.
I didn't wanna do it.
You made me cry, dear,
And all the time you know it.
I bet you always knew it . . .

See what I mean? It's catchy, that middle part, but it doesn't *explain* the story. *That's* in the opening.

Anyway, in an hour we have the song worked out. I haven't yet learned that you're supposed to do something with the left hand. The melody is all Daddy and I need at this point. When we've played it through a couple of times to make sure our stops and starts are in sync, we work together on remembering the words. He starts the song, misses a word.

"Not 'our' . . . I think it's 'my'," I offer.

"Yeah, you're right. It is," he agrees.

One more for our collection.

I'm six. Company's coming for dinner.

"Arlene, come in the living room," Daddy calls. "This is Mr. and Mrs. Fierstein. From the club. They lost their son in the war. I told them you'd play 'Boy of Mine.' Go ahead. Play it for them."

I play. And sing. Daddy joins in. From behind I hear weeping. I play the song through and swing around on the piano bench.

"Thank you, Arlene," Mrs. Fierstein says, wiping her eyes.

Daddy wants to lighten things up a bit, so he says, "Arlene can play anything. What's your favorite? If she doesn't know it, just hum it and she'll pick it up."

They name a couple of songs, mostly German ones. After "Du, Du, Liegst Mir im Hertzen," I go into some Strauss waltzes and then "Ich Liebe Dich." Now the Fiersteins are singing along and beaming.

"That's really something, Julius!" Mr. Fierstein is mopping his forehead with his pocket handkerchief. "How did she learn to do that?"

"By ear. She plays by ear," my father explains.

"I'll never forget this evening," Mrs. Fierstein says to me with tears in her eyes. "It's a wonderful thing you did for us, Arlene."

I'm not sure of *that*. I made the lady cry. How could the playing be so wonderful? I thank her and let her kiss my hand, which she does with great tenderness. Later, in bed, I take a look at my hands, with their bitten nails and the eczema patches that itch a lot. I don't understand what exactly I've done, but I know one thing: It means something to people.

I start going into the living room every day to fool around at the piano. A melody pops into my head and I figure it out on the keyboard. Only the right hand at first. I practice making the notes sound the way I'm singing. I like the two to go together, my fingers with my voice. I hear a difference between the way "Stout-Hearted Men" and "Five Foot Two" sound on my records and at the movies. Sometimes I want only the ragtime stuff; other days, all Daddy's favorite light opera songs come to my mind, and I play an hour or so of those. Depends on my mood. I don't know much about this business of moods, but I sure feel good after a session of banging away at whatever's popped into my head. And the living room is hardly ever used, except when company comes, so I have it all to myself for as long as the playing goes on.

EVERY TIME DADDY AND I TAKE A DRIVE, we pass the time with singing at the tops of our lungs. Daddy starts off, and I pick it up. By now I know his entire repertoire by heart, words and all. We have little tricks we do with the songs. Sometimes we sing the same melody at the same time; other times we alternate, line for line, or introduction for refrain. We try to sound like the songs feel, sentimental with sweet falsettos, or rough and gruff with jazzier tunes. We have a ball, I in the back seat leaning over his shoulder, almost choking him with my arms, to get close to our music, until Mother tells me to let go and sit down.

One day we latch onto something different. "Look what happens," Daddy says, "when you sing 'Five Foot Two' and 'Sweet Georgia Brown' at the same time."

"What happens?" I am definitely interested in what can happen when we try something new.

"Just listen. I'll sing 'Five Foot Two' and you come in when I nod my head."

So he starts singing with a pretty slow tempo and I watch for the nod. When it comes, I'm ready. I start "Sweet Georgia Brown" and hold my ears so I won't get off the track with his singing. *It's amazing!* We're singing two different songs-—two different sets of words-—and we're finishing at the same time! What do I know about *keys*? How come I use the same one Daddy started in? The question never occurs to me. It's just the most spectacular discover, that if you time it right so that your music lines even out all the time, the two songs sound wonderful together!

"See what I mean?" My father is really excited. "You can do that with a bunch of songs, and it's the same thing. Try . . . "

We try blending our voices with other songs, racking our brains to come up with ones that might fit together. More often than not, we hit them right, and soon it's "Here's one, Daddy," and "Now let's do . . . " and all the time, Mother, sitting next to Daddy, is listening. She's not as excited about the whole thing as we are, but she's not complaining either. It comes to my mind that two songs together have more meat on them than one at a time. From then on, I start to substitute the piano melodies for Daddy's voice, and I come to find that piano almost as good a musical companion as Daddy . . . but never *as* good.

THE YEAR I TURN NINE, UNCLE BEN, Mother's brother, marries Aunt Frances, and they move up the block from us. Aunt Frances is cultured. She has a big grand piano and she speaks perfect French. I take 'cultured' to mean 'interesting', which of course it does, in a way. Being by myself most of the time, except when I'm in school, I take to spending a lot of time at Aunt Frances's. She shows me her doll collection, the series of children's books she has placed in her bedroom bookcase, and the jewelry she keeps in her night table drawer. "You may play with whatever you like, Arlene," Aunt Frances says in her Katherine Hepburn New England-accented voice. So while Aunt Frances is in the kitchen cooking dinner for Uncle Ben, I explore without any imposed limitations like I have at home, where even the kitchen is out of bounds for me. I cannot understand how Mother allowed a piano to be placed in the living room. Must have been Daddy's doing, at least in part.

If you know the old brownstones, you can see that if someone is in the kitchen, someone else can play a piano in the front room and it won't bother anyone. After a few months of poking around at Aunt Frances' I go over to that grand piano, lift its lid, and slide onto the tufted bench. It's a tight squeeze. Think of how narrow those bay windows are in old brownstones and you'll laugh at how tough a time I have placing myself properly at that Baby Grand.

The only piece of music on the rack is entitled, "Casey Jones." Now I can't read notes, but I can read the words written under them. And of course, I already know the melody. So I start singing and playing, and no one is paying any attention because no one is around to hear me. That makes playing all the more special. If I *do* try things out and they don't work, no one will be disappointed. I won't be spoiling anyone's good time except my own.

When I grow tired of "Casey Jones," I look around for some more music. Inside the piano bench I find a fat book entitled *Your Favorite Songs*. There's a gold mine of things in that book, like, "My Gal Sal," "Indian Love Song," and so on. Before long I've learned a lot of lyrics I never knew before, ones that even Daddy doesn't know.

AT UNCLE BEN AND AUNT FRANCES'S PLACE one Thursday afternoon, the whole family arrives for Thanksgiving dinner. After the feast, everyone gathers in the front parlor.

"Arlene, play something," calls my father, who is smoking a cigar and holding a glass of Cognac. It's not a big room, and we are a fair-sized family. There's Uncle Jack, Aunt Anna, my cousins Audrey and Harris, Aunt Eddy and Uncle Martin, their two daughters Chickie and Janie, and of course, my parents and me.

As for Daddy's suggestion, I can't recall anyone seconding it, but I don't wait to take a poll. I just get out the music book, open it to "Sheik of Araby," and get going.

"What's that you're looking at?" my father asks, meaning the music book.

"I got the music here," I explain.

"You can't read music," snarls my cousin Audrey, who is eight to my ten and really, *really* hates my guts.

"What does she need music for?" my father chimes in. "She can play anything already. Who wants to hear 'The Dying Swan' from those music books anyway!"

"I can *too* read music," I protest. "Wanna see me do it, Audrey? Just watch!"

"Never mind," she says.

"*I* do, darling," calls Aunt Frances. "Play 'When You're Smiling.' It's somewhere in there."

I find it and play.

"The child reads music," my Aunt Frances announces. "At least she's playing the right hand. I can't make out what she's doing with the left one."

I am doing what I will do for the rest of my life. I am making chords that I hear from the melody, two notes together with my left hand, pressed at certain intervals that my ear tells me are right. The only difference between this time and at future playings is that I will be able to fiddle around those left hand chords faster and fancier, with the eventual help of the ukelele symbols marked over the melody notes in "fake books," those special books used by guitar players to indicate the chords to go with the melody lines of popular songs. But for the moment, there in the brownstone parlor, everyone is highly surprised at what I'm doing—just surprised, but not entirely *pleased*, mind you. Not Audrey, who can't stand me, nor a few of the grownups who can't hear what they're saying over my playing. But when I look over at my father, I see he has a twinkle in his eyes and doesn't seem to give a hoot about what anyone else thinks.

THE JACKSON DEMOCRATIC CLUB is having its annual Christmas party.

"You're old enough to go, so get dressed up," my father insists.

But Mother isn't too keen on the idea. She is dressed in a bias-cut gown of rose moire and looks like Carole Lombard, which, of course, is the idea. "She's only eleven, Julius, and besides, she has homework."

"Never mind the homework. She'll have a good time," he says. Mother gives in and I go.

The party's in full swing at the Club. Daddy pushes me through the crowd to a back room, where the bar is set up and there's an old upright piano in a corner.

"Play some Irish songs," he whispers in my ear.

"Maybe they don't want me to, Daddy. There's so much noise already." I'm feeling really out of place among all those grownups, many of whom I know through my parents, but not in this kind of setting.

"Go on," Daddy insists. "Just start playing. They'll quiet down."

My father seems so sure of it, so I make my way over to the upright. No one's paying attention to the kid getting on the piano bench, so I decide I'll just play a couple of songs and that'll be that. I start with "Danny Boy," my foot on the 'soft' pedal. I'm really getting into it, lost in the music, when I notice a couple of men looking in my direction.

"Who's that?" a tall, white-haired gentleman asks no one in particular.

My father moves over to the piano. "Hello there, Ed. That's my girl Arlene. She can play anything you want."

The gentleman leans over the piano and watches me for a moment. "You're Julius's little girl, eh? And you play the piano? Well, that's swell, now isn't it?"

My father puts his arm around the tall man's shoulder. "Arlene, I want you to meet the Honorable Ed Flynn."

"Very pleased to meet you, Mr. Flynn." I stop playing and shake the white-haired giant's hand, thinking that I've heard the name Flynn before but can't remember where.

"Little girl, can you play 'When Irish Eyes Are Smiling'?"

I start to play and Mr. Flynn sings in a terrific tenor voice. It's as quiet as a concert hall, except for some murmurings and some ooohs and aaahs. Names are called out in introduction. I learn that Judge Martin Frank and his wife Ann, who is, I think, very beautiful, are over by the bass side of the piano. Leaning on the treble side is Judge Albert Cohn, with his son Roy, who is home from college for the holidays. Roy, according to his father and mother, is a genius and will go on to a great career. (I hope they weren't around years later to see him become pompous, the acolyte of Senator Joseph McCarthy and by his side at the HUAC hearings). People come and go all evening, while Dad whispers suggestions for more songs to play while giving me quick rundowns on which names belong to which faces.

"Try 'Sweet Rosie O'Grady.' It's Maldwin's favorite song. FDR just made Maldwin transit commissioner." Sure I know Maldwin and his wife Mattie, whom I call Uncle Maldwin and Aunt Mattie. Aunt Mattie is a schoolteacher, and, without children of her own, has taken a really deep interest in me, even having the *Congressional Record,* a daily publication of everything going on in Congress, sent to me. I could never really get into it, could never understand its contents, and so the pile of *Records* has grown to become a huge stack stored in my closet. But Mattie will be the greatest influence on my education all through my early life.

As for "Sweet Rosie O'Grady," I succeed in playing it, though I'm having a serious problem: The bunch is singing so loudly that I can't hear what I'm doing. That's the same as cutting off an arm of a violinist. When they say that a person has an "ear for music," you'd better believe that the expression is really true. Put some outside sound between my head and my fingers and the circuit is broken.

Just when I'm about to call it quits—anyway, I see that my father is engrossed in a conversation with this tall kid, Roy Cohn, who's wearing his black hair plastered straight back off his forehead and parted in the middle, and whose eyelids look at half mast—I feel a poke in the middle of my back.

"Hi, Arl. They brought you too, huh?"

Relief sweeps over me. Someone to talk to. My cousin, Edmund Dollinger, who's nine years old and looks adorable in a tweed suit with knickers and a tie.

"I'm hungry as a dog," I whisper in his ear. "What's there to eat?"

"There's soda and hot dogs in the other room. Are you gonna sit here all night?"

"Where's your father?" I ask Edmund. Ed's dad is a congressman and so Ed is used to this scene, but I'm having trouble with the smoke and the smell of scotch. We're about the shortest people in the place, getting the least oxygen. "Who's gonna take us home? We have *school* tomorrow and I'll never get up in time!"

"Dad's somewhere with Mr. Flynn . . .*Boss* Flynn."

"Boss of *what*?"

"Dad says he's the boss of the Bronx."

"What's *that* mean?"

"Beats *me*."

I'm feeling dizzy. The oxygen level is definitely low at this end of the Club. "Let's get some food," I say, pushing back the piano bench and wedging my way off it. Someone's hand is on my shoulder. I take a look behind me and there's Boss Flynn. His other hand is on Edmund's shoulder.

"Well now, you're going to vote straight Democratic, aren't you? How'd you like to play at next year's convention? You'll have almost a whole year to practice the song. You *know* the song I mean, don't you?" I don't and I say so.

"Julius," Mr. Flynn calls to my father over the heads of ladies with marcelled hairdos, "tell your little girl the name of the finest American song."

My dad comes over pretty quickly.

"Let me have a word with her, Ed." Dad takes hold of my elbow and leads me back to the piano, leaving Edmund behind.

"Listen, Mr. Flynn would be pleased as punch if you showed you know our song. Here's how it goes . . ."

My father is banging on the top of the upright. "Ladies and gentlemen of the Jackson Democratic Club, Arlene dedicates this next song to our leader and a swell guy, the Honorable Ed Flynn!"

I turn around on the piano bench and play a soft C so I know where to start. This is for Daddy, the swellest guy I know.

When I go into "Happy Days are Here Again," with Daddy singing near my ear to cue me ahead, the entire crowd begins to sing, with as much spirit as any cheering I've ever heard. Some of them raises their glasses to Mr. Flynn, who towers above them. Then a few of the ladies kick off their shoes, wrap their arms around each other's waist, and do a chorus line routine, while the men clap, cupping their palms together to make the loudest sounds. They go through the song three times over, and then the party's winding down.

Dad says, "Play 'Should Auld Acquaintance be Forgot'," and I play it, with everyone swaying, arm in arm, to the slow beat of the music.

I do not get to play at the next convention, though Mother is one of the delegates from "That Great State of New York." I don't mind. I've had my fill of being in the political limelight.

IT IS MY GYM PERIOD AT JUNIOR HIGH SCHOOL 98, otherwise known as Herman Ridder. All the girls, in their green gym suits, are paired off for square dancing. I am practicing the crossed-arm promenade position with Honey Lou Liebowitz, my partner, so that when we get to that part we don't strangle each other.

"Arlene, would you mind playing 'Turkey in the Straw' for the class?" Miss Springer, the gym teacher, calls, her whistle dangling from its lanyard around her neck.

I play. Everyone is do-si-do-ing and getting the lead out of their thighs. I know this because I hear the stamping, but I am facing the gym wall and can only guess what the steps are like. I am well on the way toward developing my permanent body shape: thin arms, bony fingers, skinny legs, and an ovate middle with matching rear end.

AT SIXTEEN YEARS OF AGE, I am a buxom lass with no lack of beaux. Thanks to the piano playing, my pectoral muscles have developed well ahead of the rest of me.

My current boyfriend, a rotund, quite balding college man, president of New York University's Alpha Pi Omega service fraternity, guides me straight from the entrance of the frat house to the room where sits the ubiquitous upright piano. There is a frat party going on, and my boyfriend wants to get the attention of the other guys. I'm to be useful here.

"Sit down," he says, wiping the bench with his handkerchief.

"I wanna dance, Jack," I protest.

"Aw, c'mon. Play the piano. Then we can dance."

"But there's a record on," I point out.

Jack goes across the room and says something to one of the guys. The music stops. Jack strolls back to me and the piano.

"Now!" He commands.

I play.

Soon everyone is hanging over my shoulder and leaning

against the back of the upright, clapping, calling out song titles, and having a ball.

"Who'd you come with?" one cute fellow asks.

"Me." says Jack firmly.

"Oh." The cute one relinquishes his place at the piano and disappears.

"Can we dance *now*, Jack?" I plead. "No one's listening anymore. They're all dancing to the records again."

"Sure. But next week, bring the fake book. They didn't know the words this time."

IT IS 1970, AND I AM THIRTY-NINE. Father is barely breathing as I sit at his bedside. On the other side of the open divider curtain there is a woman huddled in a heavy coat, watching a still form in the next bed.

I see that my father's lips are very dry, and so I walk around the bed for the water pitcher and a cup.

"Would you mind waiting outside for a moment?" I turn to see a nurse standing at the foot of my father's bed.

I leave the room and wait outside the door. It is very quiet.

In less than five minutes the nurse summons me. "You can come in now. I'm sorry, but Mr. Joffe is gone."

I enter the room. My eyes sweep over my father's form. His face looks the same as before. I have the urge to hold him in my arms. I sit down on the bed, next to him.

"Please don't make noise . . . don't cry . . . my husband can't . . ." The woman in the heavy coat is speaking in a whisper to me. I understand and nod in compliance.

I lie down next to Daddy, my head touching his. Slipping my arm underneath his head, I cradle him against my chest. I stroke his silver hair, his cool forehead. I stroke his cheek while I sing him to his rest. The lullaby that raised his first consciousness of life will bring him full circle.

> *Rozinkes mit mandlen.*
> *Sleep, my little one, sleep.*

"Sing, Arlene," he may be saying after all.
I sing.

< 15 >

LAST DAY

The last day of anything
is not the *last;*

That is,
it's not the *very* last of
something that has had
a life a while—

that is,
that *you* have called
a *thing,*
some *thing*
that you are glad
or sorry has now ended

maybe *much too fast*—
you'd say—or better still,
at last.

I hope the latter's
how you view
a thing gone past.

Oh, you will see the shadow
of it—not the ghost, I hope;
and you will hear the echo

of it—not a hollow
warning.

(I would not wish
anything that's past to
make a hollow warning
sound.)

So hanging
round your life will
be that *thing* with
Last Day
tacked onto it
in memory,
but softer.

I can comfort you with this:
It will not scream
into your ear,

This is the lastday
lastday,
lastday . . .

but will whisper
that it *was* a thing,
but is not *now,*
yet still was *something . . .*

Still is.

NO FAIR

If you get off on victory,
there's plenty opportunity,
providing *you* define
the terms of battle.

But suppose you set it up
and no one wants to play?

The best that you can
hope for is a draw.
But that would be
defeat.

So now you vow,
one finger pointing
up to Heaven
(As if only He and you
could understand)
to call the whole thing
off,

as you won't be
humiliated like
that anymore!

WORDLESS

Ask me a question. I'll try
to answer it succinctly,
then move from one thought
to the next in illogical order.

I am never clear, so filled
with trepidation, fear of
being wrong:
too liberal,
naive,
incomprehensible.

No use: my words are
scattered in the murky
atmosphere, without the
aid of nouns to lead the
questioner from A to B.

I have qualified my thoughts
with multipliers by the dozens,
breathless dots and dashes,
parenthetic phrases,
weak parentheses,
to no avail.

Use your nouns, my husband

kindly offers.

Put in the hearing aids, a
helpful daughter offers.

I know just what you mean,
a tactful friend tries hard to
offer a way out.

I'm not so willing to excuse
myself. *Just keep your mouth
shut, will you!*

Late in the evening, thinking
how to find the right approach,
I write a poem that says it all.

AND SO I MUST

Where my poetry,
My *self* in perpetuity,
exists, you cannot go.

Be prepared,
while we are laughing
over something that
we've shared,

to see my eyes
take leave of you,
your face, the very
space I've occupied:

The only thing
I'll tell you is,
I've gone into my well,
and down, and down,

beyond the laughter,
down before what
happens here, beyond
the joy of love,

beyond the curtained
words like *dear* and

< 21 >

I love you, down
beyond the very limits

of what present words
can say:

This day will pass,
and I and you
and each and every
touch and taste
and smell will
one day mingle
with the air.

And so you understand
that I must go beyond
and down and on, till *everything*—oh,
everything, is gone.

SURROGATE

Someone you hardly
know gets beaten on
the street

and there is always, *always*,
someone to applaud it
surreptitiously,

not out of spite—
not *always* that—
nor something
equally or more
benign,

but for the sheer
relief of knowing
anybody,
anybody—
makes no difference who—

was the target
this time,

and for once,
that target
wasn't *you.*

< 23 >

CLEANING UP

There was the secret that you'd kept
wrapped up so tightly in the middy
blouse you had to wear to school.

They never dreamed that it was there,
or cared at all, not having access to the key
which you had hidden in that mothballed closet,
where it would be safe.

In later years, predictably,
it all came back to you,
not in a wave of shame, but with relief,
remorse, and then the task
of *what to do*.

*Keep it hidden like the silence
in that house,* like *the cat o' nine tails
hung up on the kitchen door, meant
to flay the evil out of you.*

Now your head begins to ache.
Your hearts beats rapidly.
You sit down on your bed
and feel depleted . . . nothing.

Hold on, you tell yourself.

Get up. Retrieve the key
from where it lies inside your heart.
Good girl. You've made a decent start.

Rout out the ancient stains and mold.
You're safe. They both are gone
and you are old.

What was this? Something known
and left in place?

But why? What for?
Can't remember anymore.

FOR WHAT IT'S WORTH

I am a girl of eighty-three,
waiting to see what H has up his sleeve
for dinner, agreeable to his menu choices.

It's been that way for thirty-seven years.
I can't imagine how he does it every day,
telling me *It's easy. Nothing to it.*

He is a boy of eight-five,
always searching for his book, a pencil,
anything he's put down out of place.
Always sure it's walked away.

I offer help in finding it, that missing
item, at which, invariably, it's there
just where he'd put it. For thirty-seven
years we've done that dance, he knowing
how to wring his hands and be distraught,
I leaping to his aid, and then,
the item found.

This girl of eighty-three cuts her own hair,
most often badly. Leaves the light on in
the hallway. Doesn't hear the water
trickling from her bathroom faucet. Speaks
too loudly on the telephone so he

can't read. She's sorry, but he says, *Nothing
to be sorry for.*

He knows her ways, and she knows his.
Isn't that what marriage is?

STAYING UP

Late in the evening, long
after Husband's gone to bed,
I stay up, planning to read my book
but put it down and start to write instead,
thinking of Leonia, my home town,

where all the richness of my middle years—
played out in joy or, frequently, in tears—
was centered; where it sang of life—
the pleasures and the sorrow, the sense of
being home at last, of being all that I was
meant to be, where past was past and peace
came over me, a time when all around me
were my own four daughters. I could never
feel alone: Four girls, pecking at each other,
bringing their small sorrows to their mother.

I loved that house, its sense of family, of
belonging, and still my heart is filled with love
and longing for those sweet days when Leonia
was our home. The memories remain, though
more than I can tell in this small poem.

TRAIN

I push into the crowded train,
book bag clutched to my chest,
stand against an old guy here,
old woman there, we gasping
for a breath of air.

I feel a pinch.
NOT THAT AGAIN!
Oh no you don't! I hiss.

Train continues to sway

and squeek and rattle, while
we're jammed and squeezed in
like a herd of cattle.

Time to act! I get into
position to do battle,

Gonna get my leather heel
into that Jerk!
Put his fingers permanently
out of work

Kicking back, I smile the smile

of sweet success.

A deep voice yells: *I seen huh do it!*
Wadda mess!

She just clipped diss nice old lady
wit' huh shoe!

Lady cries, *That was a mean, mean_thing to do!*
Turning semi-swiftly
to my rear.

I assess the situation.
It is clear

That the clever culprit
lurks two rows behind,

Wearing Raybans
and pretending to be blind!

He dashes out at what
I know is not his stop

Rats! My retribution is a flop.

READY

Summer

Wait, I am not ready yet.
I have so many things to do
before you come for me.

See that tree beyond the deck?
The feeder filled with seeds?
The clay pots ready for
their summer blooms?

They all depend on me,
and it is almost time
to do my part in nature's
scheme.

Give me time to see
the season through,
and when at last the beauty
fades at summer's end,
I'll gladly say good-by
and come with you.

Fall

Now the scrappy squirrel

will arrive to feed on morsels
left by bluebirds, grateful
that the fall has come.
The least that I can do is
keep the feeder filled with seed.
Who else would care?

Please wait until
my eyes grow dim, my legs
no longer usable,
the sounds of morning
muted to my ears,
and I no longer able to
fulfill my role.

Winter

Now, I beg you, wait again:
It's such a short time since
my love has gone. I need
some time to dream of him,
to see the traces of him
everywhere, to whisper
to his pillow that I love him,
miss him, long for him so deeply
that I want to die.

Then, I beg you: come for me.

BIRTH MOTHER

It was hinted
that you were a whore
and I just like you . . .
Protecting you, at twelve,
I could not issue a denial
nor a confirmation of
the charges, lacking
evidence.

I wonder what I would have
hated in you, Mother,
reaching adolescence . . .
Stranded in a womb-like
state, I made of hate
an arbitrary exercise.

We both were teachers in
the Bronx. Did you do
English? Elementary?
High school? I've done
them both to cover all
the ground between us.
I am, I think but can't
be sure, what you would
have liked me to become . . .

There is a room, Mother,
at the public library,
where you and I are bonded
in a book. We do exist
together, in that book of
1931 birth records. Some-
one did record our genealogy,
one fleeting moment between
birth and death.

If you are alone and old,
I would not mind being your
eyes, being your child again.
Being the last thing you see
before the darkness closes in on us.

What color did you dye your
hair when it turned gray?
I wear my hair this way
because I think you did,
or do. I can't say *do* to
anything. Can you?

Bear with me a moment:
Asked how many pregnancies
you've had, you pause an
instant while I flash across
your mind. You flick the
thought aside, subtract the
image from your count, but
whisper, *and Arlene.*

Four times I bore you inside
me, named Cara, Cindy, Dana,
Liza; knew with certainty the
mole under your eye, the olive
skin, dark eyes, big-knuckled
hands, and mesomorphic frame.
Four times I did commit myself
to you, a pink-wrapped bundle
in my arms, and never wavered
in my love. How could I ever
doubt that you'd loved *me*?

When you held me, Mother,
did you look at me?
Imprint your daughter's face
upon your memory? Then you
would know me, Mother,
instantly. You would.

Tracking you down is as insane
as suturing a cobweb.

I have no sounds but gray mews,
Mother. Sometimes when a laugh
erupts from somewhere deep,
untouched by you, inside me, I
am startled hearing it, find
the sound of it unsettling, and
that feeling, as if standing on
one foot forever, is much safer,
understood far better than a
burst of laughter, thanks to you.

You are my cancer in remission.
The fear of my returning to what
I once called *my real origin*
lies like heavy tissue grown
around my sensibilities. You
are contagious, and the mask
I wear is mean to keep me
sterile and remote. Like *you,
goddammit!*

And there it is: an end with no
beginning. Made it up, I did,
for old times' sake, for some
sake other than my own. And
now, direct me to your church,
your temple, mosque—whatever,
where I can perform our penance,
light the candles, say *yiska,
salaam*. Which, Mother?

In time, the clouds move on
when we no longer fix them
with our mute, unyielding stare—
when we slip out from under them . . .

HUSBAND

She'd brought him home
to show him how he
couldn't hope to fit:
That was the point of it.

His hearty laugh rang
hollow, like a cry of
pain from deep inside
a tunnel avalanched.

She wrapped herself
around us, warm and
comforted by birthright
blanket,

while sparks flashed
from his marriage band.
He clutched his fist
around it to embrace
the cutting pain.

He was somebody's child,
from some small town
where girls like her
were not aspired to,

while she was ours, our
child grown comfortable
with city people, city
lights, the razzle-
dazzle drama-comedy,
the family quilt of
vivid colors and wild
stitches.

Comfortable within that
razzle-dazzle, making a
cocoon spun of the
family yarn, she'd
brought him home, this
husband kept at bay,
and we were at a loss
to comfort him, or
say we understood.

There were no sides
to take, no sage advice
to give. *Would he
smile or weep,* we
wondered, fearing both.

UNFOLDING

Like the unfolding of a flower,
a child grows,
season by season,
according to its climate,
side by side with other blooms
not of its type.

The child can weather this,
understand what is expected:
Kindness. Love.

In the field,
though other blooms
lean this way and that
against the pull of wind and soil,

This child can keep its balance,
never veer against the elements,
hold on tightly,
knowing,
feeling
what its roots have taught:

Its time to flower lies ahead.

KATE'S BOY

Kate loves her boy
with a venom.

He is fifty years of age,
she seventy-eight,
yet she still tries
to set him straight.

He is her career,
her role in life,
her punishment
for having been
his father's wife.

LEGACY

Swimming in sweet terror
Is how I knew to be,
When currents changed
And waves rose high,
Crashing down on me.

A legacy of dread and gloom
Infused my heart and mind,
No heroine, I bore the brunt,
But finally resigned.

It was a way of drowning,
Giving in to every wave,
Not knowing how to counter it,
How better to behave.

If understanding its effect
You absolutely must,
Then think of it as part
Of an irrevocable trust.

SOLDIERS

Down along the streets of anywhere,
you listened hard for laughing kids
who used to run across your path
just for the fun of it, while you took
some offense.

Now you know what has become of them:
their cocky grins, thumbs up,
eyes hard as steel and soft as love,
looking out at you from TV screens
and small-town dailies.

Still they run across your path, your memory,
despite the hell of it, and step aside,
 look back, and smile, with the utmost
deference.

MOTHER

Looking at your baby for the first time,
you wonder how you made this perfect child.

Seeing how fine its hair, how sweet its lips,
you wonder how *you,* so *ordinary,*
produced this miracle,
and think: *I* am the mother.

Did you hold the baby in your arms
and feel your life has just begun,
its meaning clear:

Everything you *are, will be,*
will want to be, beyond the need
to be SOMEONE?

I tell you that you'll feel the same
in fifty years and more,
when both of you have gone beyond
those early roles, now
speaking as contemporaries,
telling what is in your hearts,
the heavy and the happy things,
the blows that life invariably brings.

Knowing now what never goes away:

the feeling that changed everything
from that first moment, that first day.

EVOLUTION

Gertrude at ninety-two,
having lost her younger sister,
looks around to find herself
in some new context.

Daughter? Wife? Sister?
None of these apply.
Gone, all gone,
these titles. Family people
gone to graves.

All is not lost:
Gertrude, at ninety-two,
is still called mother,
grandma, great-grandmother.

But what is left to do?
To be? To play a role?
Yes, to live for them
is still an option:
Keep the titles going
for their sake.

Forestall the day
when their turn comes
to live in memories
attached to marble stones.

THAT CERTAIN THREAD

Drawn into the web,
you bring your baggage
to that certain thread, deposit it,
put out your shingle:
Victim.

< 46 >

CALL IT LUCK

Call it luck.

Such opportunity may never
come again, when God, how
hard it is once settled in
to make acknowledgment
that you are prone to webs.

Make application, sight unseen.
Have your belongings ready,
stapled to your psyche,
ready to move in as soon as
there's a vacancy.

You *know* the cost is high,
the lease too long,
and *anyone*—oh yes, admit it:
there is nothing left to lose—
and *anyone* can get it
for a song.

WHITE

It's dark now,
wind howling,
winter imminent.

Weather channel
says snow this week.
My leg joint warned me
of that very thing.

I am a regular forecaster
with a degree in age.
White hair.
White snow.

Better not go out
lest I disappear
in whiteness.

All the same,
winter coming,
old age coming,
so much to do
in preparation.

SUN ALSO SETS

Along the Gulf of Mexico
Hemingway and Mary
took the catboat out.

The waters
pooled a green
that he insisted
looked like Dominguin's
new cape.

But Mary, chafing from
the reference, snarled,
"More like something else . . .
Oh, I remember: like his eyes."

They mused on that,
the catboat gently rocking them
together and apart,

as all along the shore
lights flickered in the dusk,
like pangs of love,
or death.

ARLENE POLLACK

TREASURES

I wander through the woods,
eyes fixed on the ground,
hunter and discoverer
of treasures:
acorns of smooth mahogany
   pine cones

Near wooden boardwalk steps
my fingers search the hot sand
where children, hurrying
to the ice cream truck,
have dropped their coins.

I am an archivist on city pavements
and grassy curbs papered with
   poignant notes
  unpaid bills
  addresses
money

near where buses stop,
and startling things occur between
people
  cars
temperaments.

Along the beaches,
when the tide goes out,
and where the sand is
brown and coarse or mud,
there are such things as
black seaweed ripe for snapping,
   skeletal remains of sea life:
   shells
bones

Look down to find
such treasures
lying at your feet.

SHE IS A WOMAN

She is a woman who,
her life stampeded to a halt,
would speak of it in terms
that indicate her innocence:

No fault of hers, that latest obstacle
put there to muddle her.

Even now, in telling of the
circumstances of her luck's demise,
she, to be sure, has others
ready—and yes, eager—
to add their woes to hers.

Then, if circumstances are in sync,
they could take in a movie
about
love
a singles dance
a trunk sale at a discount,

or even buy a dress for the
inevitable blind date.

TILLING

Don't pack the dirt down hard:
The weeds push up and you are
more surprised than if you'd
made some room for them to
raise their ugly mugs and
waited sweetly, patiently,
with tools in hand,
to do them in.

CLANK

Clank!
I pull a chain down.
Out pours links of all
my past experiences.

It is a job
to reassemble them,
but then I do experiments,

combining baby fat, sex,
a dozen Mallomars devoured
when I was seventeen,

mixed with a dozen sets of
genitals once loved,

and if I had the chance again
to pull a chain from somewhere
out of vision's range,

I'd do it in a minute, just to see
what's in it for
a gal of eighty-three.

EYRE FARE

MR. ROCHESTER HAD THE APPROVAL OF THE EYRES. We don't hear much about it from Charlotte Bronte, but Mrs. Eyre was kind enough to turn Jane's correspondence over to this author—thought it would shed light on the exact circumstances of her daughter's relationship with Mr. Rochester.

"She would have wanted to set the record straight," Mrs. Eyre explained to me. "You see, Bronte took a a great deal of license with the actual events—never did take into account Jane's heroism in all of that. And Mr. Rochester was a really terrific guy, he really was.

"Bronte just wanted the story, wanted to make it something that was pure Gothic. But it wasn't like that at all. Jane was your average young woman trying to find herself. She didn't have much confidence. No one at that age does. The crying, whining, sitting on her bed with our best china scattered around the room, full of pudding and lemonade . . ..Well, you know teenagers, I'm sure.

"The letters tell it better than anything I could say. The only one who could do the story justice is Jane, but the doctors at Eathmoor feel it would be dangerous to dredge the whole thing up. Take the letters, read them, and you'll have the truth in all of this."

"But where can I reach you if—"

"Oh, we'll be on the Riviera for the winter. There's a marvelous tennis crowd there. It sounds callous—leaving when Jane is ill—but life must go on, you know. I'll be in touch from time to time."

With that, Mrs. Eyre rose and picked up her raccoon coat from the floor. There were tears in her eyes. "Plain Jane, we used to call her. I know they say it's all in the genes, but to this day I wonder what I did wrong. You might say I've given you these letters to show how much more noble she was than I could ever be."

I needed something more to go on, something that would make me know the person whose intimate correspondence I was about to study. "Wait, Mrs. Eyre. Please. Tell me more about your daughter, something that will enable me to read these letters with a greater understanding of Jane. After all—"

Mrs. Eyre turned to me. "Listen, Buster, I'm depending on you to go public with the *real* Jane Eyre, not that simpering priss they'll teach about in English 101! Oh well . . .

"Jane'd been . . .um . . . *fragile* all along. Then *this* came up. The job, that is. Of all things, Jane loved children best. We never thought she'd marry. Being an *au pair* seemed a decent way to make a living. And she was really drawn to Mr. Rochester's little girl. But then the letters came. . . ."

You'd like him, Ma. He's not your average type. Like, he's never made a pass, and it's a year already!

"And another . . ."

He's asked for my hand, Ma, and I said okay. He's moody and goes out a lot, but what the heck! I'm thirty-five.

My luck's running out."

"A year later she wrote again . . ."

> You won't believe this, Ma, but the nut upstairs is not his mother. She's his wife! I never thought I'd be in such a spot. He's gotten weird. Sometimes I think he's got a thing fo her. She's really gross, crawling on the floor and eating food with her hands! The other night I opened the door of her room to get a good look at her, and she lunged at me! I got out of there just in time. Mr. Rochester told me never to go near that door again. He's so considerate, so patient, so sensitive . . . .
>
> Ma, I have a favor to ask. Can I come home?

"We didn't hear from Jane for a couple of months. I figured it was for the best, since we'd made her room into a sauna. She wouldn't have understood. But then, another letter arrived . . ."

> I've gone through hell the last few months. Poor Mr. Rochester was accused of murdering that lunatic! I don't want to go into the details of that mess, but he told me everything—her breakdowns, the drinking, her stay at Eathmoor to detox.
>
> Now for the good news. Mr. Rochester beat the rap! Also, he's gone through the 12-step co-dependency encounter sessions at the monastery, and our marriage counselor assures me that he's coming out of it. And that guy keeps thanking me for saving his life! Can you beat that!

Mrs. Eyre watched my reaction to this last letter. "What feeling do you get," she asked, "if you don't mind telling me?"

"That poor, poor girl," I replied. I felt I understood Jane as one understands a close friend, although I had met her only through her letters. As for Mrs. Eyre, I confess I had some doubts as to her motives. My instincts soon proved correct.

"Poor girl, my eye! 'No brain' is more like it! How would *you* like to bring up a loser and have to sit by while she lives with a creep and gets herself into one disgusting mess after another? To tell the truth, I was grateful that at least she'd had the decency to send letters instead of coming home crying, shaking, being depressed, sitting on my lap and calling me mommy and telling me everything in real time? A letter you can put in a drawer, but not a daughter!"

I couldn't believe my ears! "Mrs. Eyre," I said tersely, "you're speaking of one of the most beloved characters in all of English literature!. Why, if it weren't for Jane, you couldn't sell your letters to the *National Enquirer*! That daughter of yours has made you famous!"

"What do *you* know?" she snarled. "If it wasn't for her, I'd be somebody *myself*, not just somebody's *mother*! Mrs. Eyre started to pick at the fur on her coat with shaking fingers. Unable to contain herself, she paced around the room, speaking in a sing-song voice:

"What does your son-in-law do, Gladys?

"Oh, he's a huge success. Has a mansion, in fact. He and Jane have three adorable children and are sublimely happy."

"And does Jane work?"

"Thank God she doesn't have to. She's content to stay at home and take care of the children."

"By the way, Gladys, have you read Charlotte Bronte's new book? The title escapes me, but everyone's talking about it."

"Uh, if you'll excuse me, Laura . . ."

"Is something wrong, dear?"

Mrs. Eyre was beside herself. To distract her, I asked if she would like a glass of wine. Before I could finish my sentence, she had swept past me, flung the door open, and disappeared.

With a feeling of uneasiness, I opened the last letter.

We can't wait to have you visit, Mommy. I've cleaned out Cassandra's room—spackled, painted, nailed the floor boards down and bleached out all the food stains. The broken glass has been removed and the dents in the wall repaired in honor of your coming.

I hope I haven't upset you. I'm so grateful to you for making me wait for Mr. Right!

How did you know, Mommy?

Love always.

Jane

THE MALOXES

THE HOUSE NEXT DOOR TO THE MALOXES' had been for sale for six months. At first, Hank Malox had kept his eye out for anyone trying to inspect the house. He found that, quite frequently, a car would pull up across the street, and one or two people would emerge, dart over to the front walk, and peer through the sheer curtains into the living room of the Wilson house.

Any such impromptu visit onto *Hank's* property would be short-lived, ending when the stranger's eye and Hank's eye would meet against the window pane. But next door this little ballet occurred time and time again. It was never the same intruders, always new peepers, singly or in pairs, or even trios— any combination of people who, after satisfying some question in their minds about the condition of the house's interior, would sneak around to the back, where the small deck and newly painted garage were situated.

IN TIME, HANK STOPPED LOOKING OUT the front window to watch the action. He had better things to do. But his wife, Chickie, kept the vigil almost compulsively. It wasn't that she cared who moved next door, she insisted. It was just that she couldn't help but wonder who in their right mind would pay the half million asking price for that old Victorian, renovated though it had been, when yuppies were looking at the mansions further up along the Palisades, and older couples who were house-hunting certainly weren't looking for four floors, fifteen rooms, and all the work that went with such digs.

Actually, Chickie *did* care. She wanted to be able to come outside to the driveway in the morning, or back to the house after work, and say hello to nice next-door neighbors. The two driveways were so close that together they could have served as one wide one, as the Alpine houses did. So she kept her eye out for any unusual activity in the way of real estate agents and prospective buyers, while her husband, who usually meant what he said and really didn't care, forgot about the FOR SALE sign on the next door's lawn and went about his business.

ONE DAY AT THE END OF THE SUMMER, Chickie was lying on the couch in the front den, contemplating the tops of the trees that seemed to fill the entire frame of its two skylights. It could appear, she thought, that they were in the middle of some wonderfully isolated forest instead of on a block which had sixty-three children and was three minutes from the George Washington Bridge. The thought delighted her. She was so glad that they had decided to renovate their own home so that there were comfortable rooms in which one could sit and relax, as she was now doing.

Chickie's eyes closed for a blissful moment. Suddenly, something made her open them. She felt as if she were being watched. But that was *ridiculous*. No it wasn't! Up there, in the trees framed by the skylight, were three people just sitting there, their legs dangling from separate branches. They appeared to be a family, for the woman and man had the young girl between them, and all three were whispering and pointing at Chickie.

Showing no interest in Chickie's open-mouthed surprise, they smiled pleasantly and waved!

Wait a minute, thought Chickie. *Those people are in the trees!*

As she leaped off the couch, straightening her skirt over her hips, the realization hit her: They were house hunters nosy enough to go to any length to check out the next door neighbors before putting their money down. She'd heard of nervy things connected with such situations, but this took the cake! She'd go out there and tell them a thing or two about invasion of privacy!

She was about to open the front door when she thought better of it. She'd open the skylight instead. Best to keep distance between herself and them.

Chickie took the long window pole from the corner of the bookcase and, slipping it into the loop that was attached to a cord, gave a yank and opened the skylight. There they still were, smiling and waving as if they did this every day. She looked up at the three tree squatters with an appropriately stern expression, her hands on her hips.

"May I help you?" she asked, astounded to find that she was using the tone of voice usually reserved for those occasions when she was at her most charming.

"Oh, no, not at all. Have we disturbed you?" asked the tree-woman in an equally friendly voice. "We really didn't mean to. We're just familiarizing ourselves with the neighborhood. We love your neighbor's house, and we're trying to see the houses around from all angles."

What a pleasant person, thought Chickie, rubbing the back of her neck, which had gotten a crick from all the strain. "Are you planning to buy the Wilson house?" she asked, hoping that they were.

"Actually, we're considering it seriously," replied the tree-man, who was wearing a dark suit and cordovan shoes. "But with the market the way it is, it takes every ounce of know-how to keep on top of things, or you can lose your perspective and fall on your face."

"Well, that's certainly true," Chickie agreed, noting that this fellow had really figured out all the angles. "Look, it's getting dark and I imagine that you're not too comfortable where you are. You must think that we're terrible hosts. How about joining us in the house?"

"Why, that would be just lovely," smiled the woman, whose pink suit appeared to be caught on a branch. "Georgette dear, say thank you to the lady."

"Thank you so very much," said Georgette warmly.

Chickie's heart jumped at the thought of having this adorable child living next door.

"Would you mind giving us a hand?" asked the woman, pulling on the hem of her skirt to free it from the branch.

"No problem. I'll call my husband and he'll have you down in a jiffy. Hank, honey, come to the front room. We have company."

Hank Malox stared in disbelief. Surely this was a joke. But Chickie gave no sign of it as she saw a cordovan shoe (possibly a size 12) reaching toward the very top rung of the six-foot ladder that had been in the driveway that morning until the primate family used it to gain access to the tree.

"We're the Pickenses. I'm Ed and my wife's Sylvia. That's Georgette, our daughter."

Ed offered a hand to Hank, but Hank ignored it and said, "If you use the very top rung on that kind of ladder, you can kill yourself."

Without responding to Hank's admonition, Ed found the

< 63 >

ground and said cheerfully, "We're *really* interested in the Wilson house. Probably going to be your neighbors!"

"You know, liability insurance is very high in this area." Hank noted. After helping Sylvia and Georgette to the Malox lawn, he hustled the ladder into the garage.

Chickie was inviting the flying Pickenses in for tea when he returned. Ed said they really hadn't ought to accept the invitation, but Sylvia thought they ought. Hank noted that Sylvia was used to winning.

WHILE GEORGETTE WAS CHASING FELIX, the ancient Malox cat, who had disappeared into the shrubbery, the Maloxes and Pickenses settled themselves in the front room to talk things over.

"What can you tell us about the area?" Sylvia asked.

"Well," Hank admitted, "it's damn close to the bridge, and there's lots of traffic in the evenings—especially on holiday weekends."

"But that's why we love it here!" Sylvia exclaimed. "Ed works in New York, and he has to take the bus every day. It's such a drag."

"Of course," Chickie remarked, "our lots are small, because we're so close. If you like to garden, it's a disadvantage." Chickie looked over at her husband, saw that he was scowling, and tried her best to help his cause and at the same time maintain an air of sociability.

"No problem there. We just love the idea of being close to our neighbors," Sylvia said, retying the laces of her Reeboks. "We feel there's enough alienation in the world. What we need is the warm support of friends and neighbors, and we in turn need to give our love and support to *them*. Don't you feel that way, Ed?"

Ed felt that way.

Sylvia and Hank searched each other's faces to gauge where

the conversation was going. Hank broke the silence. "And of course there's the radon."

Ed, catching Hank's words, whispered, "Radon?"

"Nothing to worry about," Chickie laughed nervously.

"I don't know who sets those government levels," Hank said from behind his hand. "We've been living here seven years and we feel fine."

"So far, so good," Chickie added.

Sylvia was looking at Ed's face. "It's a lot of money for so small a lot," he remarked, staring off into space. She nodded in agreement.

TEA WAS SERVED. The Pickenses made polite excuses and left, and peace once again reigned at the Maloxes. While Chickie mopped the milk that Georgette had spilled on the rug, Felix cautiously emerged from under the rhododendrons.

THAT TASTE OF DENTYNE

FELIX CAPRICORN STARED INTO Mrs. Klapsich's open mouth, pur- posely avoiding her eyes, which he knew from experience would show no amusement, no friendly security—just terror.

"How's everything?" he asked in a jocular tone.

"Aghulch," Mrs. Klapisch replied.

"Glad to hear it," Felix said, bringing his nose closer to her cheekbone. "Well, we're going to give you a new smile. You know, your jaw has been receding for a very long time. We'll straighten it all out. A little bite-builder, some root canal work on that pivot tooth, a couple of implants and bondings. You won't recognize yourself afterwards."

Felix felt safe in turning his gaze upward to meet Mrs. Klapisch's. He wanted to see her reaction to his message. Her eyes were squeezed shut. Had she heard?

He decided not to pursue the answer to that question. Let the piped in music of Morton Gould do its work. "Tornem a Sor- rento" seemed to lull patients into a blissful state in which there was no teeth, no dentist, only romance.

STRETCHES OF
THE IMAGINATION

Driving sixty
miles an hour
away from you,

I hypothetically
shift into reverse
and double back
along the phantom
highway,

to where you
wait for me,
hypothetically.

ON NATURE

On autumn days, before
the winter settles in,
and leaves have fallen
from the trees to make
a carpet underfoot, he
rises early,

gathers up
his gear, then drives
alone to where the
nature lovers walk
the trails.

There among the foliage,
he spies a bird he's never
seen before and wants to
know what bird that is,

wants to know whose
company he's keeping,
here where TV sets and
state-of-the-art computers
hold no sway,

where man is the
observer, not the

< 68 >

predator,

here, where dappled
sunlight plays along the
water and where birds
are not afraid that he will
do them harm,

he, with his binoculars,
tripod, long-lensed camera and
(they know this well from
long experience with him)

the keenest eye
and best intent.

FRIENDS OF MY YOUTH

Friends of my youth,
there was a time
when you were all
to me, and now I've
learned you've gone.

That's to be expected.
As the seasons come
and go, all nature carries
on within its given time,

and what we loved to see,
and touch, and smell, and
call *our* tree, *our* blooms,
live with us until they
wilt and die.

Now I am old, and more
and more I think of you,
my dearest friends of
long ago, remembering
how we grew together,
blossomed in so many
ways that marked our
time together.

I remember it with love.
The years go by, we change,
and yet the *heart*, the *heart*
does not forget.

AGAIN

It was happening again,
that slow unraveling
of skeins they called
their life together.

Often there was
desperation for some
change, a sense of
strangulation, coming on
not all at once, but slowly.

Then he'd say, *All right,
I'll do it for your sake
because I love you*—

meaning, *Look, we
might as well. We're
stuck together like two
pigs in glue*—

meaning, *Face it, the scabs
take longer to fall off,
and we are out of patience,
out of time.*

They knew, of course, that

this was not the last of it,
this feeling or this conversation
or this making peace
with what, for them, they
knew was love.

< 73 >

STILL COUNTING

Counting who has gone
or who still tangos,
I see it is too late
to say *Goodbye*,
I'm sorry.

Some I left.
Others left me.
It doesn't matter anymore,
and who would care?

Now the play is
 in its final act.
Time to say *good-bye*,
so long, see you later.

But honestly,
I wouldn't count on it.

SIMON WINTER

1
Simon Winter was plucked
off the city streets
against his will.

The crime was age,
the sentence: madness.

Some said it was
about time Simon quit.
What man of eighty-five
stays on the streets that long?

Simon never did respond,
strapped to a pallet
on the tile floor of
an isolation room,

writhing,
gagging,
chanting
in a singsong voice
those syllables-on-syllables,

his body bouncing off
the cinder block,

with the compliance of
a burly guard who's
seen much worse.

In a second's passage
from the teeming streets
to airless cavern, Simon's
dreams spilled, snaked,

contorted in that cell
where old men are
deprogrammed

like the precious,
gathered,
stored-for-
next-time data
when computer's down.

2
It took two years for all of
Simon's cells to empty—
Mama, Papa, Ida, Minnie,
little Rose,

the tailor shop on
Second Avenue,
the greenhorn schoolboy,

papers on a floor just scrubbed,
a brother's death—
from his mind's

accounting book,
evidence of life
once lived,

the sweetness
and the gall of it.

Gone the boardwalks.
Gone Atlantic City,
Rockaway,

the avenues where he was known
and welcomed into shops
that smelled of sawdust,
fish, black olives,
sour pickles,
home-baked bread,

out of the cell into the rooms
that held him to some place
in time,

where feeding, bathing,
dressing, scolding,
medicating

went on and on
until it was
the all of life:

Long white corridors
with wheelchairs

facing wheelchairs.

3
Simon Winter spent
a thousand days
strapped in a chair,

his head bent low,
his silver hair gone
wild and tangled,

mouth gone slack
for lack of words
to protest or demand

or even whisper names
of ones he loved
and who loved him.

4
Who holds the book
of Simon's life
and Simon's death?

Who holds the message that
his living mattered,
and his dying too?

I do.

TESSIE

Tessie isn't coming anymore
to feed and bathe old Mrs. Cross
who knows that Tessie didn't
really do *that* much—not half
as much as Mrs. Baron's girl
Felicity.

Tess would always say
before she left at five,
when Mrs. Cross was
finished with her snack
of buttered toast and tea
with milk and sugar
on the side,

Now you be sweet, dear,
and I'll see you soon,
 God willing.

But Mrs. Cross thought
Tess's saying to be sweet
was mean, because she was
already sweet as she could
ever be, and no one had
to say those words to her,
especially not the girl.

< 79 >

ARLENE POLLACK

Well, Tess got sick,
or so her husband said,
and when she got around
to calling Mrs. Cross

she said she wasn't
all that sure about when
she'd be back because
her arms and legs
were hurting so.

I'll try to come tomorrow,
Tessie said, but Mrs. Cross,
wise to the ways of girls
like Tess, knew that she'd
never come, because they
never do once they say that,

and wasn't it a nasty thing
to do, to leave her all alone
without her bath, so helpless
and so sweet as she was—
had been—all her life.

Tess never came again.
Now someone else gives
Mrs. Cross her bath,

and makes the little snack
at five o'clock,

but never says "God bless you,"

with a kiss upon her cheek,

and never says "Be sweet"
like Tessie did.

< 81 >

FROM A FATHER TO HIS SON

I wished for a long life
and here I am, now eighty-five,
still wishing, wanting still,
to walk in stride with you
and hold your hand,
stepping over pebbles
and the soft white sand
that hold the sea at bay,
wishing to rescue you
from some misstep
beyond the water's edge,
needing to shelter you,
to dare a tidal wave
to pull you out to sea.

I am your father.
That alone does not enable me
to smooth the way, protect you,
nor to guide you through
the life you've made.

Yet, since the day I held you
in my arms and fell in love,
I cannot shake the feeling
of your being mine forever,
of watching you from

< 82 >

some point on the sand,
my little son, as you walk
out into the vast unknown.

The course of life
has put you in my place
as keeper of your own dear ones,
with whom you travel
on their own terrain,
the shell-encrusted beach
along the vast and swirling sea,
Ready to pull them safely back.

Turn your head, my son, to see
this eighty-five-year-old
who, standing far behind,
still watches over you
with outstretched hand.

DEVIL'S DUE

Nothing that we do
is not linked to
that already done:
our wretched history—

nations' competitions,
cold war tactics,
birth and deaths of
heroes and of scoundrels.

But these have been
exposed by scholars,
researched, understood,
forgiven.

Not so the links
of family history
that lie so deep
below the native soil

that only holocausts
or celebrations
rout them, flaunt them,
make our agonies
out of the myths we tout

but never research,
understand,
forgive.

< 85 >

KNIGHTS OF THE TIMES TABLE

The Knights of the Times Table
raised their goblets high, in
recognition of their leader,
Loco, whose sole motive was
to expedite the clan's planned
routings with the utmost speed.
And it was they, the Knights,
who shared their Loco's motive.

"Let us, on this occasion,
pay great tribute to each noble
knight, for knights are noble,
are they not?" demanded Loco,
letting off some steam.

The Knights, who never were
adverse to blowing their own
horns, agreed in unison *tout
de suite*. "Indeed they are . . .
we are . . . aw, they sure are!"

"I fear, my men," said Loco,
chug-a-lugging his great
stein of mead, "you all are
bored. But let us keep our course,
for Heaven's sake!

"Sir Charge, our Keeper of
the Coffers, 'tis to you we owe . . .
We owe . . . oh, I forget just
what we owe, but owing to
your brave accounts of
enemies encamped upon
our hills of Beverly and
Forest, we were able to
discharge those ruffians and
thus set the record straight!

"And you, Sir Tax, have been
a veritable right arm to you,
Sir Charge, and both of you
are owed much gratitude for
spreading our prestige
here and abroad.

"What say *you*, Sir Cuss,
known to all for your good
humor and your ribaldry,
parading an array of lions,
tigers, dancing girls and
such, to give us courage,
and thus keeping us on track?

"Ah, we have not forgotten that
among us at one time moved two
who are no longer at our table,
for they could not bridge the
gap between base human nature
and nobility. I speak of Sir

Lee and Sir Pent, those common
men of forked tongue and some
devious intent, who tried in
every way to influence our
mild Sir Tenley to betray
his vows. But did you fall into their
trap, Sir Tenley? Not at all,
I say.

"Shall we go on to greater
victory, my noble knights?
Give me your answers!"

"We shall, without Sir Cease,"
the knights replied, now raising
their mugs on high. "He
stopped to tie his laces and
was captured by the Serbs."

"It serbs him right!" a voice
intoned.

"Who is it that hath made a
mockery of one of our
anointed?" Loco railed.
"It was Sir Plus," a voice
called out. "We've had
enough of him, with all his
bragging and his gathering
the spoils of every victory!"

"He's been no asset to us,"

Loco said. "He lacked the
motivation. We could well
have stormed the palace of
that evil monarch, King Key,
if Sir Plus had not been busy
with some what-nots strewn
about the grasses on the vast
King Key estate."

"That's so," called out Sir
Ian. "But, good knights, let
us retire in the knowledge
that we have among us all
the bravest, truest men in
this great land!"

"And the cutest," lisped Sir Gay.

"Aye, 'tis so." his comrades all
agreed, and with a final tootle
from their drinking horns, they
clanked in single file out of
the hall, with their beloved
Sir Gay following behind.

< 89 >

BEFORE THE ENLIGHTENMENT

Gay students I have known and loved,
What will become of you?
To love with all your heart another
soul is all you need to know of
life's intent.

I have seen you in the psychiatric wards,
divested of the shards of glass that you
employed as punishment,

and I have watched you ache
for proferred kisses and caresses,
searching for the wellspring of
that alien desire.

I have played your songs,
accompanied your voices,
sweet with tenderness,
making love in adolescence
through the words, their
messages discreet enough
to suit your time.

I have seen you venture
from behind your camouflage,
so tentative and so alone,

amidst your proper families,
so helpless to allay the passion
emanating from a mirror image—
breast to breast and genital
to genital, so drawn to sameness.

I have seen your faces at my door,
alone or arm in arm with your new
mirror friends, to show me that you
have finally become yourselves—
so proud, so peaceful, after family
storms and other vanquished trials,
Herculean from the war and wanting
to affirm my part in it.

And I have seen you dying—you, and you,
and you—and gone to your memorials,
and heard that you have left behind a
grieving regiment of peers who pledge
remembrance.

And I have heard your families speak
with pride and love for what you were
to them.

There was no talk of how the
mechanisms worked when you made
love, but only that you gave love
and received it too—at last, but just
too late.

OLD PHANTOMS

Old phantoms
never hang around
without an audience,

normally
keep late hours
and a low profile,

unless the host insists

< 92 >

FOCUS

Sit down with me
  Amidst the rubble heap
Of life's fond dreams
  Abandoned or destroyed,

And place upon the ground
  Before us all
The strategies for living
  You've employed.

With great precision
  Let us test them out
For evidence of premise
  That fell short

Of reason,
  Possibility,
To see what joy,
  What sorrow
They have wrought.

What is the solace
  That we hope to find
To clean away the stains,
  The bitter marks,

Our indiscretions,
  Loathsome memories,
Like blight that covers
  Nature's pristine parks?

Sitting there
  Upon the rubble heap
You now insist
  That it is your life throne,

Built of solid gold
  And strongest steel,
A monument to you
  And you alone.

Perhaps the vision
  That you have is real,
And that which scratches me
  Is not debris

Molded into warped
  And hurtful things;
Perhaps you feel them
  Cushions; that could be,

For does it really matter
  What has passed?
And will analysis
  Reveal the way

In which we moved
  Circuitously toward

The point at which
   We find ourselves today?

Agreed: The rubble heap
   Is no such thing—
Instead, a bed made of
   The softest fleece,

Where we may re-
   Invent the past
In order to assure
   Our present peace.

IN TEN YEARS

In ten years,
most likely we'll be gone—
we who studied Shakespeare,
we who understand and speak
the Romance languages,

understand and read
the Russian novels,
know what quatrains are,
and Middle English,

understand the fugue form,
movements of the classic symphony,
contrapuntal music,
and the past indefinite.

In ten years
they will use the present perfect,
make their observations short and sweet,
declare the history of Mankind
no older than two generations,

and wonder how we came to
our out-of-date conclusions,
yet survived.

RANDOM OBSERVATIONS

1

Yesterday is a shop we frequent,
for its wares are, on the whole,
appropriate. We do not buy the
whole place out—only what we
think we need for our today.

2

Pile up the images that haunt us.
Now smother them with antidotes:
the memories we have of bravery
and our finest moments. There.
The sun reflects our vast collection
like the light revealing threads of
pure spun gold within a rougher cloth

3

There is a word for everything
that makes us cringe or fills us
with the utmost joy. Behind the word
existed first the feeling. We are,
therefore, not unique to anything
that has necessitated the assignment
of a word. We are involved in common
practice, not in unique loneliness.

4
At one end of a passage is a word,
whose meaning reverberates along
the passage at whose end exists the
door where we unlock its antonym.

5
In our time, there is a set of
every kind of thing. We rarely get to
know one tenth of what has been our
time. And yet, we want to know about
a time before, long come and gone.
How poor we are at living.

6
We are not half as wide as a train;
Not one hundredth as tall as the
tallest building. But we make our-
selves the center of the universe,
blotting out the larger scheme
of things.

7
We spend our lives finding ourselves,
when we would be so much richer
by losing ourselves.

8
Gain is a word that measures money
and weight. Loss also. Both words
are conspirators in inverse ratios.
That is part of our ethic of absolutes.

9

We want to be remembered in the
fondest way by those who have
been given so little of the
best of us.

10

We are moved by great causes, and
willingly donate to worldwide
charities, for these are easier
to deal with than the immediate
agonies around us.

11

We readily record the sensibilities
of the self, but rarely spend ten
pages of our diaries on the other.
Our journals are, in every sense,
spiraled.

12

We do believe in capital punishment,
the kind we mete out to ourselves,
for we do not trust the judgment
of those who know us well. And
yet,we rail against a system that
believes in punishing the vicious
criminal, because he is a human
being, after all, and who are we
to judge?

13

People who don't think they're
anything at all are free to
start anywhere at all. The rest
of us, who've gotten somewhere
and are something with a title,
are stuck with it.

14

Whatever we have lost was with us
for a while, which, given the finite
nature of everything, is something
to be appreciated and stored as future
energy, not be the cement of our
torn spirit.

15

Dust is a test of our farsightedness.
Do we triumph over it by turning
our eyes toward things that move
and carry us away in flights of
fancy, or do we settle for routing
it and feel a satisfaction in the
recognition of its being, some-
how, the enemy?

16

We fill our surfaces with pictures
from the past, and while we beam
upon them from our favorite chair,
the subjects captured in the frames
go on to grow and change, beyond

our living room. We have not captured
time; it has captured us.

17
The snapshots of a favorite trip
eventually lose their energy, for
they reflect what was once done.
Just that.

18
Some of us are lightning rods for
flashes of emotion; others of us
are lightning rods for grand
inspirations. Whatever. Let's
not forget that lightning rods are
out there in position to be struck
by something, and to synthesize
the energy

< 101 >

FAUN

Let's pretend
you are a faun
and I am an exotic,
running through
the forest, where
you lie in contemplation
of your world.

I am dressed in
silk, a flowing
scarf, a garland
in my hair, and
in a flash, as I bend
down to pick an
acorn from the ground

you leap at me,
posturing and weaving
in and out of my
 small space. Of course
I notice you. What
can I say? You are
a faun, while I,
mother of four, am
merely gathering
herbs for dinner,

< 102 >

I, tired from herding
children, see that
you are gay, leaping
back and forth
and laughing.

*Come home with
me*, I say, *and we
will have good
coffee and a slice
of my homemade
bundt cake.*

I notice that you
hesitate, then raise
your ram's horn to
announce you'll be
away forever from
your old and mossy
haunts, to be
forever mine,
my joy,
my husband
for a lifetime,
yet, and always,
faun.

DISINTEGRATION

When that bond
disintegrates,
you fill in time,
change course,
set to the newer
task, and say a
somewhat
tentative
goodbye,

like spring leaves
gone to brown,
like things that
lived a while
until the season's
change, then
quietly,
inevitably,
flutter down.

WHAT'S THAT, YOU SAY?

They talk a blue streak
slurring their words as if
to hide them from our ears,
not sure that I'd agree
with what they have to say.

They never realize
that I don't get it:
hearing's not acute,
and then they speak
too fast to boot.

I nod and smile,
hoping they'll want
to stay a while.

Then, when a lull sets in
they make their getaway,
promising to come again
another day

to make me smile,
expecting me to say,

That would be wonderful.
Oh, by the way—
what did you just say?

< 105 >

RUNIC'S TUNIC

Across the vast Alarak Swamp, where myron birds and gypple toads lie in wait for the devious kankeree,, Mistral Mester and his flock of bobbats wait too, motionless, for the glees to come.

There is a sobbing in the air and the swirling of sin . . . Meela can hear it . . . feel it. She lifts her wetmop to the skies and intones:

> *"Ah, ye byrdes and lothsom antes*
> *With ye whelping, gros infantes,*
> *Here I wait, yeself a-cummin',*
> *Horns a-plenty, wilde drummin'.*
> *Yo la la, falah, falai.*
> *Fetch me here, and ye shall die."*

"Mistral Mester, when think ye the glees shall swarm?"

"When the kankeree has shed his winter skin, Lady Meela."

"Come now, Mistral Mester, 'tis but January. The winter clime's a-buddin."

"Then I shall make preparation for the Thankesgivin' and let bygones be bygones."

"Reckon I shall do the same, and see thee in three monthes'

time."

Meela picks at the lint on her wetmop. "This waitin'," she moans, "is makin' of me a fool.

The glees shall come in their goode time, and yea will I."

> "Sonna shine and pritty flores
> Shall grow tendre at our doores.
> On our swamp the glees will singe.
> Ah to hear their voices ringe!
> Ho and hey and ribald runder.
> Is the stew full done, I wonder?"

Meela makes two circles with her wetmop and squints at the climeless skies. It is not yet time, and time is all there is, and mortals must keep faith with faeries whilst the swamp curdles.

The glees would be pleased.

BEGINNING

Into the light, I came,
bursting forth,
umbilicus attached
to Mother,

she who, sobbing,
understood that
what she'd done
was right:

that love,
its fruit, this living
thing.

And now to sleep,
to rest the mind,
close it to regret,

and yet this product
once inhabiting her
womb would prove
to be tenacious,

prove to be too
deeply meshed

with flesh that,
molded with the
living proof of
love, would not,
could not erase

His face, would not
escape disgrace,
the bond that
birthing brought
to her, to me,
neither of us free,

the Mother and the
Child, the faceless She,
the orphaned Me

FLOW

Alone
and lonely.

Sorry state.
Nothing now
to celebrate.

No one here
to call a buddy.

Mind so empty.
Thoughts so
muddy.

Body wants
to eat and sleep.

Feel so hopeless
way down deep.

Wish these blues
would go away.

Nothing else
for me to say.

< 110 >

Nothing
else
for
me
to
say . . .

< 111 >

www.ingramcontent.com/pod-product-compliance
Lightning Source LLC
Chambersburg PA
CBHW051811040426
42446CB00007B/626